THE LAST DAYS OF STEAM IN
NOTTINGHAMSHIRE

Bill Reed posing alongside Class 4F 2-6-0 – Ivatt locomotive no. 43040, working on a local ballast train. The locomotive was built at Horwich Works in 1949 and was withdrawn in November 1966. The picture was taken during the early 1950s while Bill was a fireman.

THE LAST DAYS OF STEAM IN
NOTTINGHAMSHIRE

From the Bill Reed Collection

PETER TUFFREY

AMBERLEY

A photograph dating from 1986 has captured driver Bill Reed in the cab of Class 20 locomotive no. 20 215 at Nottingham Carriage Sidings before leaving, light engine, for Calverton Colliery, which opened in 1953. The Colliery was closed by British Coal in 1993 but reopened soon after under the ownership of RJB Mining. The colliery finally closed in late 1999 and the buildings were demolished in February 2000.

First published 2010

Amberley Publishing
Cirencester Road, Chalford
Stroud, Gloucestershire, GL6 8PE

www.amberleybooks.com

Copyright © Peter Tuffrey, 2010

The right of Peter Tuffrey to be identified as the Author
of this work has been asserted in accordance with the
Copyrights, Designs and Patents Act 1988.

British Library Cataloguing in Publication Data.
A catalogue record for this book is available from the British Library.

ISBN 978-1-4456-0306-3

Typesetting and Origination by Amberley Publishing.
Printed in Great Britain.

Contents

This book is dedicated to Jonathan Mark Lewington
(30/1/1995 – 7/5/1997)
The boy who loved 'choo-choo' trains.

Acknowledgements

I would like to thank Bill and Mary Reed for their help and support throughout the project and Alan Sutton for having confidence in the book once again. I would also like to pay tribute to the wonderful work done by the various individuals behind www.wikipedia.org and www.railuk. info. Special thanks are also due to Malcom Crawley, John Wayman and Pete Washbourn.

Introduction

Bill Reed's interest in railways goes back to his early childhood when his mother used to take him to visit her sister in Hucknall, travelling from Bulwell on the Sentinel Steam Railcars no. 5192 *Rising Sun* and no. 51908 *Expedition*. However, he has been told that even before then his paternal grandfather took him to see trains at Bulwell Common. His grandfather was a retired driver, formerly on the MS&LR at Northwich, who came to Annesley to work on the GCR when it opened. He moved his family to Bulwell in order to get promotion to become a driver. Bill's father was also interested in transport, having been apprenticed at Broughs, the Bulwell motorcycle builders, and after the Second World War he worked at Wrigley's Wagon Repair Works.

Growing up in Bulwell, Bill was always aware of the rail services, with such a complicated network and so many stations. In fact it was a young trainspotter's paradise. His father had an allotment, conveniently situated at the side of the Great Central line, and overlooking Bulwell Common Sidings. He bought his first stock book, Ian Allen's *ABC of British Locomotives,* in 1943, which he still keeps among his treasures. On Sundays he regularly met up with a group of railway enthusiast friends and they cycled from Bulwell Common to such places as Annesley, Kirkby, Toton and Colwick. He spent his holidays trainspotting, tripping to places as far afield as Scotland and Devon.

When Bill left school, the only job he could find with the railways was as a messenger lad at Nottingham Victoria Station enquiry office, earning 39s a week. This enabled him to travel to and from work on the local train from Bulwell Common. He really wanted to work in the motive power department but was too young. Work as a messenger lad was varied; one of his jobs involved packing posters and handbills to all the local factories. Sometimes Bill got the opportunity to answer train enquiries and so became familiar with railway timetables. He still keeps up an interest, finding himself answering enquiries and helping friends to plan Continental and American holidays.

Bill spent his lunch hours on platforms at Victoria Station where he first met Freddie Guildford, a well-known local railway enthusiast. He knew all the Colwick drivers and many others too. His enthusiasm was infectious. He encouraged Bill to take photographs, but the latter's only camera was a Kodak 127 with perforated bellows. Freddie also showed Bill how to develop films and make contact prints. Later, Bill bought an Agefold two and a quarter square camera, which was really only suitable for still photography.

By January 1950 Bill was getting fed up with waiting for a transfer to Annesley Loco Depot, so he went to the Midland Region at Middle Furlong Road. There he was immediately able to obtain a job as an engine cleaner, the first step in the long slow haul to be a driver. The progress was interrupted by National Service, when Bill was drafted to the Royal Corps of Signals and sent to Singapore. While he was there he bought a Kodak Box Brownie and then an Agfa Isolette III. He joined the RAF photographic club and although the membership fee was expensive for him on Army pay, he managed to afford it for one month, the time it took him to make enlargements.

Bill enjoyed guard duty at the Singapore military hospital since it was at the side of a main line with passenger trains to Kuala Lumpar. He photographed at the shed in Singapore, but he was reminded of home when passing through the Suez Canal, seeing a Class 04 2-8-0 and an 8F 2-8-0 working trains.

On being demobbed Bill bought an Agfa Super Isolette, which in 1955 was considered a very good camera. He has used it to take most of his collection and still sometimes uses it today. Bill returned to work at British Rail as a fireman, and besides firing on normal runs to such places as Crewe and Wellingborough, he went on excursions to Cleethorpes, Blackpool, Dudley Zoo and South Lynn. Sometimes it was necessary to lodge overnight at railway hostels. Generally, the locomotives he worked on were 4Fs, 8Fs and Class 5s. In 1966 he was passed for driving, but had to wait thirteen years before being made a regular driver. By that time, steam had given way to diesel.

In later years, most of his black and white photography was done with a Mamiya 330, but he also had 35mm Practicas, a Canon for colour, and a Bolex 8mm cine.

Bill's interest in railway photography has taken him to all countries of Western Europe and most of the old Eastern bloc, where he had his fair share of excitement, photographing through open toilet windows on trains and from under bushes during the years when photography was totally forbidden; he even got arrested in Czechoslovakia.

He has crossed Canada on CN and CP routes and also travelled extensively in the USA. He had an ambition to see all the remaining Union Pacific 'Big Boys' 4-8-8-4 articulated locomotives, and has now seen most of them. His journeys have taken him to Denver, Cheyenne, Los Angeles, Chattanooga, St Louis and many other places travelling by Amtrak or Trailways bus. In Chattanooga, he had a footplate ride on 630, a 2-8-0 Baldwin of the Tennessee Valley Railroad.

Fortunately, Bill's wife Mary shares his interests. They met during 1966 when they were both involved in filming *A Year in the Life of the Sheriff of Nottingham*. Mary comes from a railway family, having had two great-grandparents working for the railways in the 1880s and later numerous other relatives working as gatehouse keepers, signwriters and locomotive drivers. Bill and Mary are both interested in foreign-built locomotives which can be found in Great Britain, and have toured extensively searching for and photographing Orenstein & Koppels, Jung, Krause Maffei etc. Presently, they both photograph main line steam. Bill says: 'It is a real treat to see the locomotives in such fine condition. It really brings back memories, though they were seldom so clean and shining in my firing days.'

Chapter One

Rambling Round

Royal Scot Class 4-6-0 locomotive no. 46122 *Royal Ulster Rifleman* passes Arkwright Street (Queen's Walk) Sidings. The locomotive was built by the North British Locomotive Company, Glasgow, in 1927 and withdrawn on 17 October 1964. Two Royal Scots have been preserved. These are (4)6100 *Royal Scot* and (4)6115 *Scots Guardsman*. No. 6100 *Royal Scot* is owned by Bressingham Steam Museum in Norfolk, and returned to steam for first time in over twenty years at the West Somerset Railway's 2009 spring gala.

Class K3/2 2-6-0 locomotive no. 61896 heads west with a Colwick–Burton semi-fitted freight train on 25 April 1960. The picture was taken at Arnold Road, Highfields, looking towards Leen Valley Junction. The Great Northern Railway Class H4 (classified K3 by the LNER) was a class of 2-6-0 steam locomotive designed for mixed-traffic work. No. 61896 was just two years away from withdrawal in May 1962, having been in service from 1930 when it was built at Darlington Works.

A modern view at Arnold Road, Highfields. Following the closure of the railway, the cutting was filled in to accommodate a housing development.

Arnold Road, Highfields – the scene today.

Heading east, at Arnold Road, Highfields, on 25 April 1960, is WD 2-8-0 locomotive no. 90288. The train is a pick-up freight from Sutton Metal Box factory to Colwick. The bridge in the background carries the former GC main line. Beneath the latter bridge runs the former GN Basford tunnel. The locomotive was withdrawn in September 1962.

Looking towards Bagthorpe Junction from Perry Road Bridge on 25 July 1964. In view is a Class 4F 2-6-0 Ivatt locomotive no. 43066, hauling three BR-built suburban coaches. The train is the 16.15 Derby Friargate–Nottingham local service. The locomotive was built at Doncaster Works in 1950 and scrapped in January 1967 at Swindon Works.

Bagthorpe Junction, from Perry Road Bridge, on 15 August 1964, showing former GWR 4-6-0 locomotive no. 7910 *Hown Hall*, running light engine from Annesley to Nottingham Victoria. The locomotive was built in 1950 and saw fifteen years' service before withdrawal.

Jubilee Class 4-6-0 locomotive no. 45735 *Comet* coupled to Black Five no. 45146, both running light engine from Annesley to Nottingham Victoria. The view is from Perry Road Bridge. *Comet*, built at Crewe Works in 1936 to the designs of William A. Stanier, spent its last months working from Annesley Shed and was withdrawn in October 1964. Engine no. 45146, built in 1935, survived until June 1965. Annesley Shed closed on 3 January 1966.

When this picture was taken from the Perry Road Bridge on 25 July 1964, Britannia Class 4-6-2 locomotive no. 70004 *William Shakespeare* was on its way to the carriage sidings just beyond the location at New Basford to pick up empty stock for Nottingham Victoria to work London to Marylebone. The BR Standard Class 7, otherwise known as the Britannia Class, was a class of 4-6-2 Pacific steam locomotives designed by Robert Riddles for use by British Railways for mixed-traffic duties. Fifty-five were constructed between 1951 and 1954. The Britannias took their names from great Britons, former Star Class locomotives, and Scottish firths. The class remained in service until the last was withdrawn in 1968. Two survived into preservation, the first-of-class, number 70000 *Britannia*, and 70013 *Oliver Cromwell*.

Rebuilt Royal Scot 4-6-0 locomotive no. 46165 *The Ranger (12th London Regiment)* is seen from Perry Road Bridge while running light engine to Nottingham Victoria to work a London Marylebone parcels train.

Class 9F 2-10-0 locomotive no. 92013, at Bagthorpe Junction, hauling an Annesley–Woodford coal train on 15 August 1964. These trains were known locally as 'windcutters'.

Basford Junction on 9 May 1965, where Class 8F 2-8-0 locomotive no. 48004 is travelling with a brake van into Basford Junction Sidings. The overbridge carries the former GN lines to Derby Friargate and Pinxton. At one time the metal brackets on the bridge supported a public footbridge.

Taken on 14 September 1963, a Derby Friargate–Nottingham Victoria local train joins the former Great Central line at Bagthorpe Junction. The train is being hauled by Class 4F 2-6-0 – Ivatt locomotive no. 43156, another of the Colwick-allocated Class 4 MT locomotives. These earned the nickname 'Yankie 4s', and one of the class has been preserved on the Severn Valley Railway. The photograph was taken from the bridge stretching over Valley Road.

At Basford North Station on 31 August 1963, B1 4-6-0 no. 61141 works a Saturdays-only Derby Friargate–Mablethorpe train. The photograph was taken from the locally known Dobbie Bridge. The line in the background, leaving Basford North, connected the former GN and GC lines at Bulwell Common.

A picture taken recently at Basford North Station showing how the location has changed.

Class 8F 2-8-0 locomotive no. 48388, designed by William A. Stanier and built at Crewe Works, is moving round the curve from Bulwell Common on 7 October 1966 with a coal train for Stanton Iron Works. The picture was taken from the Brooklyn Road overbridge.

LCGB, The Midland Limited Rail Tour, headed by Class J11/3 0-6-0 locomotive no. 64354, approaching Basford North Station on 4 October 1962. Basford North railway station was opened originally as Dob Park Station, as it was built on land belonging to that estate, but quickly changed its name to Basford and Bulwell. Built by the Great Northern Railway (Great Britain) on its Derbyshire Extension in 1875-76, and later again renamed Basford North to avoid confusion with the Midland Railway's earlier built station (Bulwell Market) that opened in 1848, it closed in 1964. No. 64354 was built at Gorton Works in 1903 and withdrawn to the same location in October 1962.

Black Five 4-6-0 locomotive no. 45232 passes round the curve to Bulwell Common on 4 August 1963, while working on a Derby Friargate–Cleethorpes excursion train. The picture was taken from Brooklyn Road overbridge.

Class B1 4-6-0 locomotive no. 61106 is hauling a day excursion train to the east coast while entering Basford Tunnel during August 1958. The photograph was taken from nearby allotments. The B1s were designed by Edward Thompson and 410 were built *c.* 1942-52. No. 61106 was built by the North British Locomotive Company, Glasgow, in 1946, and its last shed allocation was 38E Woodford Halse before being withdrawn to Darlington Works in November 1962 and cut up.

4-6-0 Black Five – Stanier locomotive no. 44691 approaches Basford Tunnel, known locally as the 'rat hole', while heading the 08.50 Skegness train during August 1960. Lines on the immediate left run to Leen Valley Junction, Colwick Sidings and Nottingham Victoria. Those in the middle lead to Basford Carriage Sidings, and the single one, far left, stretches between Bagthorpe Junction and Basford North Station via Basford Tunnel. Dobbie Bridge is visible in the background.

Class O4/1 2-8-0 – Robinson locomotive no. 63587 entering Basford Tunnel with a mixed freight train. The London & North Eastern Railway (LNER) Class O4 initially consisted of the 131 ex-Great Central Railway (GCR) Class 8K 2-8-0 steam locomotives acquired on grouping in 1923. The engines were designed by John G. Robinson and built at the GCR locomotive works at Gorton, Manchester. The LNER rebuilt many, allotting them into eight subclasses. O4/1: Introduced 1911: Robinson GCR design with small boiler, Belpaire firebox, steam and vacuum brakes and water scoop. The O4 class was used to haul heavy freight trains.

Class B1 4-6-0 locomotive no. 61141 entering Basford Tunnel, tender first, while working an empty stock train between Derby Friargate and New Basford Carriage Sheds on 5 July 1960.

L1 Class 2-6-4T locomotive no. 67760 on the Pinxton–Nottingham local train, 25 March 1960. Note the GN somersault signal at the 'rat hole' entrance. The LNER Class L1 was a class of 2-6-4T steam locomotives designed by Edward Thompson. The prototype no. 9000 was built in 1945, but the remaining 99 were built under British Railways' control in the period 1948-1950. No. 67760 was built by the North British Locomotive Company, Glasgow, in 1948.

A special train from Mansfield to Dudley Zoo, headed by BR Standard Class 5 4-6-0 locomotive no. 73136, leaves Basford Vernon Station on 4 August 1963. The locomotive belongs to the group numbered 73125–73154, fitted with Caprotti valve gear. Basford, Old and New, was well served by railways with no less than three stations bearing its name in one form or another, Basford Vernon (its first) was built on the Midland Railway's Nottingham to Mansfield line.

Class 4F 0-6-0 – Fowler locomotive no. 43951 on '38 trips', shunting in Basford Vernon Station Sidings. The station closed on 4 January 1960. The photograph, like the one above, was taken from the Church Lane overbridge during June 1963. The factory in the background belonged to a local dyer.

Shunting in Bestwood Colliery Sidings on 18 July 1957 is Crewe-built Class 4F 0-6-0 Fowler locomotive no. 44151 with fireman Charlie Hill looking out of the cab. The overbridge in the background carried the former GN line to Newstead.

On 9 July 1966, Black Five 4-6-0 locomotive no. 44825 took a Railway Enthusiasts Club special train of brake vans (for enthusiasts to ride in) from Trent Station to the Calverton Colliery branch line. It is pictured here on a section of the route where the line in the foreground leads to the factory of Bayles & Wylie.

Class 8F 2-8-0 locomotive no. 48141 is seen on a ballast train on the link line between the former Great Central main line and the old Great Northern Line at Bulwell. In the background, on the left, is Bulwell Common Station Bridge, with a signal box to the right. The other locomotive, which is just visible, in the middle background, is on the former GC line. The driver of 48141 awaits signals from the Permanent Way staff, while their inspector is seen with his hands on his hips.

The modern scene at Bulwell where, since the days of steam ended, the track has been removed and new houses erected.

Grimy BR Standard Class 9F 2-10-0 locomotive no. 92095 clanks and hisses at Bulwell Common, while passing the down distant signal (for Moorbridge Junction), and heading for Linby with a train of empties from Woodford Halse. The line depicted here ran parallel with Bestwood Road as far as Moorbridge Junction. On the other side of Bestwood Road is the former Midland line to Worksop. The viaduct, on the right, carried the old GC main line north from Bulwell Common. The man starting to climb down the embankment is the late Gordon Hepburn, a well-known railway photographer. The tracks and underbridge have since been removed.

At Bulwell Common Station down sidings, on 10 July 1965, is Class 04/2 2-8-0 locomotive no. 63644 with a coal train bound for Stanton Iron Works. Bulwell Common Station closed on 4 March 1963. There is a goods shed to the left beyond the signal box, and Rigley's Wagon Works may be seen in the top right section of the picture. Most of the area depicted has since been redeveloped.

Coasting downhill at Arnold Road on 18 August 1962 is 9F Standard Class 2-10-0 locomotive no. 92096 on the old Great Central main line, working a southbound mixed freight train (probably from Annesley to Woodford). While the bridge in the distance still exists, a new housing estate covers the cutting. The locomotive was built at Swindon in 1957 and saw ten years' service before withdrawal.

Class A3 4-6-2 – Gresley locomotive no. 60054 *Prince of Wales* approaches Bulwell Common during May 1957, with the up *South Yorkshireman*, travelling from Bradford to Marylebone via Nottingham Victoria. Towards the end of the steam era, the train was hauled by a Standard Class 5 locomotive. The picture was taken from Bulwell Golf Course.

Perhaps the largest physical reminder of the Great Central Railway's existence in the Nottingham area was the Bulwell Viaduct. It cut Bulwell in half and could not be missed when entering the town from the north. It therefore came as something of a shock when, after standing rail-less for some twenty-one years, a decision was taken to demolish it over the 1988/89 Christmas period. The old Midland line that stretched under the arches is still in existence and for some time served only Calverton Colliery. The latter's closure over the 1988/89 Christmas period gave the contractors the opportunity to take possession of the line. The picture shows rubble from the viaduct being removed.

On its way to Bulwell Common, while heading north from Nottingham Victoria on 18 August 1962, is Standard Class 5 4-6-0 locomotive no. 73069. The engine is hauling the 10.20 from Hastings to Sheffield Victoria. This position at Arnold road was one of photographer Bill Reed's favourite locations for taking pictures.

In the 1950s, former North Eastern (LNER B16) locomotives, like the one seen here, were quite often used on Banbury–York freight trains. York-allocated locomotives were the norm. Class B16/1 4-6-0 locomotive no. 61477 is seen just north of Bulwell Common Station on 11 June 1957, working a Banbury–York express freight train.

Class B1 4-6-0 locomotive no. 61288, on 24 August 1959, at Bulwell Common, heading a Nottingham Victoria–Sheffield Victoria local train. The picture was taken from Bulwell South Junction signal box and also shows the connection on the right to Basford North.

At Arnold Road during August 1955, Class B16/2 4-6-0 locomotive no. 61457 passes with a Sheffield Victoria to Nottingham Victoria local train. Towards the end of passenger operations between the two cities, the time taken to travel by this route was considerable; the seemingly short distance of 38 miles took two hours and five minutes. The service closed on 5 September 1966.

On the former GN connection from Annesley via Bestwood, B1 Class 4-6-0 locomotive no. 61285 approaches the north end of Bulwell Common Station on 18 April 1964 with a Rotherwood–Colwick mixed freight train.

Class V 4-4-0 Schools – Maunsell locomotive no. 30925 *Cheltenham* was caught piloting Class 2P 4-4-0 – Fowler locomotive no. 40646 at Bulwell Common on 13 May 1962. It was hauling the RCTS *The East Midlander*, a Nottingham Victoria–York Enthusiasts Special. No. 30925, designed by Richard Maunsell, was built at Eastleigh in 1934. The locomotives were named, from 1930 onwards, after public schools of the south of England, initially due to their proximity to the railway that served them. This proved to be another successful publicity campaign by the Southern Railway. The class-naming process included pupils from the relevant schools visiting 'their' engine during the naming ceremonies. No. 30925 was withdrawn in 1962 and is preserved as part of the National Collection at the National Railway Museum, York.

Passing Bulwell Common South Junction with the 09.00 Sheffield Victoria–Bournemouth Central on 31 August 1963 is Royal Scot 4-6-0 Fowler/Stanier Class locomotive no. 46126 *Royal Army Service Corps*. The picture was taken from Bill's father's allotment near St Alban's Bridge.

Class 9F 2-10-0 locomotive no. 92011, built in 1954 at Crewe, passing Bulwell Common South Junction on 4 March 1963 with a York–Banbury fully fitted freight train. The two lines behind the locomotive lead to Basforth North. The land beyond the embankment formerly belonged to the railway and was rented as allotments, though it is presently occupied by bungalows.

The most frequent service at Bulwell Common Station down line was not advertised to the public, but was nevertheless quite popular. This was the staff train from Bulwell Common to Newstead Station, situated near Annesley shed. The service received the nickname 'DIDO' meaning 'day-in-day-out; the train ran through the day and night – even on Saturdays and Sundays. The DIDO seen here, on 12 June 1956, at Butler's Hill, is being hauled by an ex-GN 4-4-2T – Ivatt locomotive of the C12 Class, no. 67363.

C12 Class 4-4-2T – Ivatt locomotive no. 67363 leaving Bulwell Common with the 'DIDO' on 23 July 1957. The locomotive was designed by Henry Alfred Ivatt, built in 1900 at Doncaster Works (GN no. 1505 later LNER 4505) and withdrawn in November 1958. A total of sixty locomotives were built and mostly for use on London suburban services, being fitted with condensing apparatus for working through the Metropolitan tunnels. On being replaced by the larger N2 0-6-2 tanks, this apparatus was removed and the class was scattered over a wide area, mainly working on country branches. No. 67363 had its boiler pressure reduced to 170 lbs and was fitted with push-pull control apparatus in 1948-1949. The locomotive was withdrawn in November 1958. None of the class of locomotives is preserved.

B1 Class 4-6-0 locomotive no. 61183 leaves Bulwell Common on 12 June 1957 with the 18.35 Nottingham Victoria–Sheffield Victoria local train. Edward Thompson who designed the B1 is probably remembered by most for the desecration of *Great Northern* and *Cock of the North*. However, his greatest success was the B1 4-6-0 which rivalled the LMS Black 5 and the Great Western Hall. Fifty-nine of the 410 locomotives were named. Early B1s were named after species of antelope, while later engines were named after directors and board members of the LNER. This meant that the Class B1 contained the shortest name given to a British locomotive ((6)1018 *Gnu*) and one of the longest ((6)1221 *Sir Alexander Erskine-Hill*).

On a Sunday in September 1961, B1 Class 4-6-0 locomotive no. 61111 is seen from locally known Half-Penny Bridge with the 14.30 Nottingham–Victoria local train.

Class K3/2 2-6-0 – Gresley locomotive no. 61856 leaves Bulwell Common on the down goods loop line during September 1957, with a train of empties for Annesley. The former GN track on the right was locally known as the 'DIDO' line, running from Bestwood and Newstead. The Great Northern Railway Class H4 (classified K3 by the LNER) was a class of 2-6-0 steam locomotive designed for mixed-traffic work. The first ten locomotives were built at the GNR's Doncaster Works in 1920, to the design of Nigel Gresley. Six further batches were built at Doncaster and Darlington Works, Armstrong Whitworth, Robert Stephenson & Company and the North British Locomotive Company. The last examples were delivered in 1937, with a total of 193 locomotives having been built.

Class 5 4-6-0 locomotive no. 45277 is travelling light engine near the locally known 'Kissing Gates' crossing at Bulwell Common during March 1958. While the golf course in the distance remains, all the railway has been removed.

Photographed from Bestwood Road on 31 August 1963, Class 4P 2-6-4T – Fairburn locomotive no. 42232 passes under the former GC viaduct at Bulwell Forest Crossing while working on the 08.50 Nottingham Midland–Worksop local train. The old Midland line left Nottingham Midland Station via Lenton and split with the Trowel line at Retford. It then went through Mansfield to Worksop.

On the former Great Central main line, a filthy WD 2-8-0 locomotive no. 90241 passes Bulwell South Junction on 10 July 1965, with an up Annesley – Woodford coal train. In the distance is Bulwell South Junction box and down sidings. The locomotive working nearby is probably on shunting duties. The picture was taken from Bill's father's allotment, now part of the Goosefair public house (renamed Sporting Chance) car park.

Built at Derby Works, to the designs of William A. Stanier, Black Five Class 4-6-0 locomotive no. 44825 passes Bulwell Forest Crossing, working a Railway Enthusiasts Club Railtour brake van special between Trent and Calverton Colliery Branch on 9 July 1966. At this point the locomotive was just over a year away from withdrawal after approximately twenty-three years in service.

Class 4P 2-6-4T locomotive no. 42089 designed by Fairburn and built at Brighton Works in 1951 is at Bulwell Forest Crossing during August 1964, with a Nottingham Midland–Mansfield local train. A train of empties is passing over the former GC viaduct and just visible in the background on the left are Bulwell Forest level crossing and box.

Bulwell Forest Crossing looking south towards Lenton on 31 August 1963, where Class 4F 0-6-0 Fowler-designed locomotive no. 44139 is heading a Nottingham 'Spike' Sidings to Mansfield pick-up goods train. In the background is Carey's factory. The driver, Les Bridgeford, looking from the cab, was to die in an accident near this location only a few weeks later.

At Bulwell Forest on 31 August 1963, Class 4P 2-6-4T – Stanier locomotive no. 42587 and BR Standard Class 5 4-6-0 locomotive no. 73140 are working a Saturdays-only train between Nottingham Midland and Scarbrough Londesborough Road, travelling via Newstead, Ollerton and Doncaster. The trains were double-headed because those stopping at Hucknall needed help starting again, due to problems caused by mining subsidence. The assisting locomotive was taken off at Mansfield. Fireman Mick Adams is seen in the leading locomotive and Pete Richings in the second one.

During July 1955, Ivatt 2MT 2-6-0 locomotive no. 46501, built at Darlington in 1952, approaches Carlton Station with the 16.15 Newark Castle–Nottingham Midland local train. In the background is the former GN line to Colwick and Gedling Sidings. The latter route is closed and Colwick Sidings is now a retail park. Carlton Station was opened *c.* 1846 and was renamed from Carlton & Netherfield to Carlton on 6 May 1974.

Class 8F 2-8-0 locomotive no. 48355 passes Edwalton Station during March 1963, with a Kirkby–Wellingborough coal train. Edwalton Station opened in 1880 and closed on 28 July 1941.

An Ivatt 2MT 2-6-0 locomotive no. 46404 at Chilwell Ordnance Depot on 20 May 1963, with a train to Elmton and Creswell via Radford and Mansfield. The man in the foreground is the chargeman of Chilwell Sidings. The branch line left the main line just south of Attenborough Station on the Nottingham Midland to Trent line. The passenger service was used by civilian workers.

BR Standard Class 2 2-6-0 locomotive no. 78020 at Chilwell Ordnance Depot on 25 May 1963, with a Chilwell–Newark train. On the website *The History of Beeston – an Overview* it is stated:

> Chilwell Shell Filling Factory ... was put together by Lord Chetwynd in a very short time at the beginning of the 1st World War to help address the demands for shells for our forces in Europe. On July 1st 1918 it was the scene of what remains the largest ever explosion in the British Isles ... which resulted in the deaths of 134 workers many of whom were subsequently buried in a mass-grave in Attenborough Churchyard. The site became dormant between the Wars but was activated to play a full part in the 2nd World War as Chilwell Ordnance Depot supplying tanks and other equipment to the front, then and in subsequent conflicts. Much of its land has now been put into residential or other use although the core of the site remains.

Black Five 4-6-0 locomotive no. 44835 running light engine past Hucknall Central to Basford Carriage Sidings on 3 April 1965. Hucknall Central Station was opened on 15 March 1899 and closed on 4 March 1963. On the *Disused Stations Site Record* website it is stated:

> Hucknall was the third station in the town and was the least conveniently sited and was never well used. Most of its traffic was railway workers catching the 'Annesley Dido' train to Annesley loco shed. The station was renamed Hucknall Central on 1st June 1923.

Britannia Class 4-6-2 locomotive no. 70013 *Oliver Cromwell* with a Special Train approaching Langley Mill Station. One of fifty-five of the Robert Riddles-designed 'Britannia' class, *Oliver Cromwell* was built at Crewe Works, being completed on 30 May 1951. Officially designated a mixed traffic locomotive, the Britannia class was primarily allocated to express passenger duties. 70013 was selected to operate the last steam passenger train prior to the abolition of steam traction on British Railways lines, and in the summer of 1968 *Oliver Cromwell* hauled several specials, culminating in the Fifteen Guinea Special which ran between Liverpool and Carlisle on 11 August that year. Following withdrawal in August 1968, the locomotive became part of the National Railway Museum's collection.

Class 4P 4-4-0 locomotive no. 41144, built to the designs of Sir Henry Fowler by the North British Locomotive Company, Glasgow, in 1920, is passing Lenton South Junction, on 11 July 1955, with the Lincoln St Marks – Derby express. The locomotive was in a batch of 195 that were built between 1924 and 1932. No. 41144's last shed allocation was 21B Bournville before withdrawal in March 1958 and being scrapped at Derby Works.

View of Lenton South Junction, looking towards Beeston, 19 September 1955.

A view from Lenton Lane bridge where Class 4P 2-6-4T Fairburn-designed locomotive no. 42185 passes Lenton South Junction on 11 July 1955, with a mixed freight train for Nottingham Sidings. The locomotive was built in 1949 and saw fifteen years' service.

Class 4F 2-6-0 – Ivatt locomotive (with double chimney) no. 43018 at Lenton South Junction on 11 July 1955, with a Leicester–Nottingham local train.

Class D11/1 J. G. Robinson-designed 4-4-0 Large Director locomotive no. 62667 *Somme*, built in 1922 at Gorton Works, is at Lenton South Junction on 11 July 1955, with a Derby Midland–Lincoln St Marks local train. The locomotive's last shed allocation was 39B Sheffield Darnall before withdrawal in August 1960. The Clifton Top Sidings are on the left, once used for storing freight trains from Clifton Colliery and Wildford Power Station. Note the lower quadrant signals.

On 6 June 1955, Bill made a special journey to photograph Black Five 4-6-0 locomotives numbered 44943 and 45274 with the Royal Train, heading towards Nottingham on the down main line. Note the Royal Train head code – headlamps on all the brackets – on the locomotive leading the train. The Dunkirk housing estate is in the distance and the field on the right has since become an industrial area.

Class 4P locomotive no. 42183 at Lenton South Junction on 11 July 1955, with a Nottingham Midland–Leicester local train.

View of Lenton South Junction on 19 September 1955. The route from Lenton South to Lenton North is on the left. Nottingham Goods Sidings and Castle are in the background. The up and down main line is in front of the signal box. A Class 4F locomotive is just visible on the up goods line.

Looking east towards Wilford Road on 11 August 1963, Class 4F 0-6-0 – Fowler locomotive no. 43918 is with a Staythorpe Power Station ash train heading to Beeston Sidings, while awaiting signals at Mansfield Junction outside Nottingham Shed. In the background on the right, the massive coaling tower of Nottingham Shed is visible. The goods yard can be seen on the left in the distance while ash pits are evident in the foreground.

On the last day for passenger trains on the line, Class 4P 2-6-4T locomotive no. 42218 passes Mansfield South Junction on 10 October 1964, with a Nottingham Midland–Worksop local train. The line on the left was to Rufford Colliery, and a connecting line in the foreground once led to Mansfield Shed.

Class J52/2 0-6-0ST locomotive no. 68851 is shunting coal wagons from Newcastle wharf loading bays near Melbourne Park (in background) on 23 September 1956. The locomotive was photographed while on loan from Colwick to Cinderhill Colliery.

A. H. Peppercorn-designed Class A1 4-6-2 locomotive no. 60114 *W. P. Allen* with a down express at Muskham Troughs on 2 June 1956. Note the water trough sign on the left. The 'X' lamp on top of the sign was illuminated at night. Built at Doncaster Works in 1948, the locomotive saw sixteen years' service. All the class were scrapped with the discontinuation of steam, with none of the original production run surviving into preservation. But in 2008 a brand-new Peppercorn A1 locomotive, 60163 *Tornado*, was completed. On the A1 Steam website it is stated: 'W. P. Allen was a prominent trade union official who began his railway career on the Great Northern Railway then became a member of the Railway Executive. Naming a locomotive after such a person rather than directors reflects the fact that the A1s entered service during a Labour Government's tenure.'

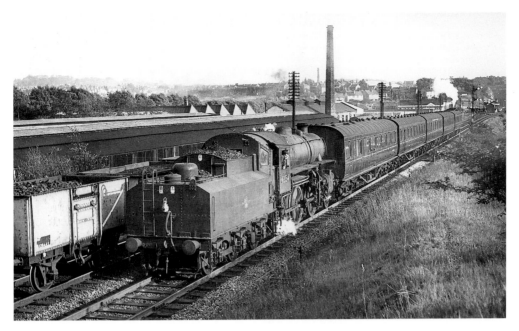

One of the regular services seen from New Basford, Perry Road Bridge, was for Nottingham Victoria–Derby Friargate via New Basford, Basford North, Kimberley and Ilkeston. Quite a few of the fourteen or so daily trains started or finished at Grantham and, on Saturdays, there were trains from Derby to Skegness and Mablethorpe. Class 4F 2-6-0 locomotive no. 43154 is one of the LMS Class engines, which was allocated to Colwick and regularly used on this service. The picture of the 17.25 Nottingham Victoria–Derby Friargate train was taken on 14 September 1963.

At New Basford on 15 August 1964, WD Class 2-8-0 locomotive no. 90383 is with a mixed through freight train to Burton.

The view from New Basford, Perry Road Bridge, after the railway was abandoned.

Black Five 4-6-0 locomotive no. 44834 passing New Basford Carriage Sidings on 14 September, with the 10.45 Poole–Sheffield express.

The view south towards New Basford would bring some hardworking engines into view. The old GC line steadily climbed all the way from Nottingham Victoria to Bulwell Common and the sound effects of the locomotives trudging uphill was something not to be forgotten. This picture, taken on 8 August 1964, shows a Colwick–Tutbury Yard train of gypsum being hauled by Class 8F 2-8-0 locomotive no. 48729.

Built by the North British Locomotive Company, Glasgow, in 1934, Jubilee Class 4-6-0 locomotive no. 45562 *Alberta* is at New Basford, on 25 July 1964, with the 10.34 Bournemouth–Bradford Exchange train. The locomotive was withdrawn in October 1967.

Class 9F 2-10-0 locomotive no. 92030 was photographed from New Basford, Perry Road Bridge, on 25 July 1964, hauling a train of empties between Woodford and Annesley. The Class 9Fs, designed at Brighton were introduced in 1954 for heavy mineral traffic. They were built at British Railway's Crewe (178) and Swindon (73) Works. No. 92030 was built at Crewe Works in 1954 and saw just under thirteen years' service.

Crewe-built Class 9F 2-10-0 locomotive no. 92011 at New Basford on 29 August 1964, with a train of empties for Linby Colliery.

Built in 1937 ex-GWR 4-6-0 locomotive no. 6858 *Woolston Grange* is seen passing New Basford Carriage Sheds, on 15 August 1964, working the 10.34 Bournemouth West–Bradford Exchange. The Great Western Railway (GWR) 6800 Class or Grange Class was a mixed-traffic class of 4-6-0 steam locomotive. There were eighty in the class, all built at the Swindon Works. Western Region locomotives were not a common sight north of Nottingham, yet, as serviceable steam locomotives became in short supply in the early 1960s, more of them were required to work further north from places such as Banbury and Oxford. No. 6858 was withdrawn in October 1965.

Taken from New Basford, Perry Road Bridge, on 25 July 1964, the photograph shows locomotives Class 4F 2-6-0 no. 43155 and B1 4-6-0 no. 61361 working the 16.35 Nottingham to Derby Friargate express. The locomotives have just emerged from Sherwood Rise Tunnel and passed through New Basford Station to run eastwards on to the Great Northern line to Derby. To see two locomotives on the GC and GN was unusual. New Basford Station closed on 7 September 1964.

BR Standard Class 5 4-6-0 locomotive no. 73159 at New Basford on 29 August 1964, with a Poole–Sheffield Victoria train. The locomotive, designed by Robert A. Riddles, was built at Doncaster in 1957 and remained in service until October 1967.

Sometimes after finishing a Friday night shift and snatching some sleep, Bill Reed would cycle to Perry Road Bridge for a Saturday afternoon photography session. In summer this would be very rewarding for him as there were numerous holiday trains to capture. On 14 September 1963, Class B1 4-6-0 locomotive no. 61088 is working on a Skegness–Derby Friargate train.

Type 3 Diesel-electric locomotive no. D6810 with the 11.16 Bournemouth West–Newcastle train at New Basford on 14 September 1963. The Type 3 (Class 37) was ordered as part of the British Rail modernisation plan and became a familiar sight on many parts of the British Rail network, in particular forming the main motive power for InterCity services in East Anglia and within Scotland. The locomotives also performed well on secondary and inter-regional services for many years. Built in the late 1950s and early 1960s, the order for the locomotives was split between English Electric's Vulcan Foundry at Newton-le-Willows, and Robert Stephenson & Hawthorns of Darlington. 309 locomotives were produced in total.

Darlington-built Class 8F 2-8-0 locomotive no. 48541 is at Pinxton, on 25 June 1962, with a train of empties for Kirkby Colliery. Pinxton box can be seen in the background. Pinxton South Station, to the left of the locomotive, was opened by the Great Northern Railway as 'Pinxton' on its Derbyshire Extension in 1875-76. In some timetables it was listed as 'Pinxton for South Normanton' and was renamed 'Pinxton South' in January 1954, closing in January 1963 with the withdrawal of all regular passenger services beyond Awsworth Junction.

No. 70012 *John of Gaunt*, a BR Britannia Class 4-6-2 locomotive, is seen here at London Road Junction on 2 September 1965, after leaving the eastern end of Nottingham Midland Station. The locomotive was working on the RCTS East Midlander–Lincolnshire Rail Tour Special. The Type 2 Diesel-electric locomotive is on the goods line. The photograph was taken from London Road Low Level Station. The bus in the background is on London Road Bridge.

Edward Thompson-designed B1 Class 4-6-0 locomotive no. 61192 is at Ruddington. The engine was built by the North British Locomotive Company, Glasgow, in 1947, and was in service until October 1962, the final shed allocation being 38E Woodford Halse.

Former LMS Class 3F 0-6-0 locomotive no. 43658 at Sheet Stores Junction (coming off the Castle Donnington Branch) on 14 October 1962, while working the Midland Limited Rail Tour between Burton-on-Trent and Derby Midland via Castle Donnington, Trent Station, Trent North Curve and Derby Midland. Designed by Samuel Waite Johnson, the locomotive was built at Vulcan Foundry in 1900, rebuilt in 1916, and withdrawn in September 1963.

Standing on the goods line at Stapleford and Sandiacre signal box (out of view) on 30 October 1955, with a train of empties is Class 4F 0-6-0 locomotive no. 44229. In the distance can be seen Toton coal hopper and the footbridge over lines to Toton Meadow Sidings.

At Tibshelf and Newton, on 15 April 1965, is Class 4F 0-6-0 locomotive no. 44420 just months away from withdrawal in September 1965. The engine had been in service since 1927. It is shown here with a coal-weighing tender.

Class 4F 0-6-0 locomotive no. 44113 working from Tibshelf Sidings with a train of empties. The picture was taken on 15 April 1965 and the bridge in the background is at Newton.

At Tibshelf and Newton, on 15 April 1964, Class 4F 0-6-0 locomotive no. 44420 is banking another locomotive in the class, no. 44113.

Class 4F 0-6-0 locomotive no. 44420 leads no. 44113 down the bank, giving extra brake power, with a coal train bound for Tibshelf Sidings on 15 April 1965. Note that 44420 has a coal-weighing tender.

Class 8F 2-8-0 locomotive no. 48214 at Tibshelf and Newton, on 15 April 1965, while climbing the bank with a train of empties on the way to Pleasley Colliery.

Class 4F 0-6-0 locomotive no. 44113 at Tibshelf and Newton.

At Trowell Summit, on the approach to Wollaton canal underbridge, during August 1966, is Jubilee Class 4-6-0 locomotive no. 45581 *Bihar and Orissa* with the Bradford Exchange–Poole Express. The road bridge in the background carries Coventry Lane. The locomotive was in service between October 1934 and August 1966.

Jubilee Class 4-6-0 locomotive no. 45664 New South Wales at Trowell Summit during June 1957, with a Sheffield–St Pancras train. Four Jubilees have been preserved, (4)5593 *Kolhapur*, (4)5596 *Bahamas* and (4)5690 *Leander* have been worked in preservation. The fourth, (4)5699 *Galatea*, was saved from Woodham Brothers scrapyard as a rusting hulk and is slowly being restored.

Gresley rebuild Class D 16/3 4-4-0 locomotive no. 62571 at Trowel Summit on 12 May 1957, returning from York with the RCTS East Midlander Nottingham Midland–York Special Train. Driver George Kelsey from Nottingham is looking out of the cab.

At Trowell Summit, during June 1957, is Jubilee Class 4-6-0 locomotive no. 45589 *Gwalior*. The Wollaton canal bridge is in the foreground.

Passing Trowell Station with a mixed-freight train on the Erewash Valley line, on 29 October 1966, is Class 8F 2-8-0 locomotive no. 48282. The station closed on 2 January 1967 and the platforms on the main line have now gone. The picture was taken from a footbridge.

Ivatt Class 4MT 2-6-0 locomotive no. 43022 passing Watnall Sidings, on 30 August 1963, with a 09.30 Derby Friargate–Nottingham Victoria train.

Stanier Class 8F 2-8-0 locomotive no. 48388 at Watnall, on 26 May 1966, with a train of empties for Colwick. The line has since been removed and the cutting filled in for a housing estate.

On the former GN line at Watnall, Class O4/3 2-8-0 Robinson-designed locomotive no. 63694 heads a Stanton Iron Works–Colwick empties train. Watnall Colliery Sidings is in the background. The view, looking west towards Kimberley, was taken on 24 September 1957 from a public footpath leading from Bulwell Cemetery in Nuthall. No trace of the railway remains with much of the area shown taken up with Local Authority and private housing developments.

Robinson Class 04/3 (rebuilt to 04/8) 2-8-0 locomotive no. 63754 at Watnall, on 11 March 1958, works a ballast train from Bulwell to Watnall Sidings.

At Nuthall, on 6 May 1957, is Gresley's Class K2/1 2-6-0 locomotive no. 61723 heading an Eastwood–Bulwell Common train of empties. In the background are Nuthall Sidings and Watnall Colliery Branch. There were ten locomotives in the K2/1 Class. No. 61723 was withdrawn in November 1959, its last shed allocation being 38A Colwick.

Edward Thompson designed Class L1 2-6-4T locomotive no. 67798 pictured, on 6 May 1957, working a Derby–Grantham train. The L1 prototype no. 9000 was built in 1945, but the remaining ninety-nine were built under British Railways jurisdiction in the period 1948-50. Withdrawals of the class were between 1960 and 1962. None survived to preservation.

Gresley designed Class J39/3 0-6-0 locomotive no. 64976 at Watnall on 24 September 1957. The LNER Encyclopaedia website states:

> The first outline diagram for the J39 was produced in September 1925 and the first locomotive entered service in September 1926. The design was very similar to the J38 and incorporated very little influence from Doncaster. All of the J39s were built at Darlington except for one batch of twenty eight J39s built between 1926 and 1937 by Beyer, Peacock & Co.

No. 64976 was built in 1941 and saw eighteen years service. This was Gresley's largest class; there being 293 in total.

Riddles-designed WD Class 2-8-0 locomotive no. 90002 at Watnall, on 30 May 1965, with a mixed-freight train from Burton to Colwick. The locomotive was withdrawn in April 1966; the last shed allocation being 36A Doncaster.

At Watnall, on 30 May 1965, working engine and brake to Bulwell Common Sidings, is Class 04/3 2-8-0 locomotive no. 63639.

Passing Watnall Sand Sidings with a mixed-freight train, on 30 May 1965, is Class 04/3 2-8-0 locomotive no. 63873.

Travelling south past Wilford Brick Yard signal box, on 25 July 1962, is Class K3/3 2-6-0 locomotive no. 61882 with an Annesley–Woodford mixed freight train. The picture was taken from Ruddington Lane road bridge; the gate on the right leads to the disused sidings at Wilford Brick Yard.

This photograph was taken south of Wilford Brick Yard and shows Black Five Class 4-6-0 locomotive no. 44780 heading the 18.15 local train from Nottingham Victoria to Rugby Central.

On the old GC main line approaching Wilford Brick Yard signal box, on 9 June 1966, is Black Five Class 4-6-0 locomotive no. 45464 with the 17.15 Nottingham Victoria–Marylebone express train. Wilford Brick Yard is in the background.

At Wollaton during August 1966, and climbing up from Radford Junction with the Bournemouth Central–Leeds City train, is Black Five 4-6-0 locomotive no. 45219.

Passing Wilford Brick Yard signal box during June 1962 is BR Standard Class 5 4-6-0 locomotive no. 73034 with a Nottingham Victoria–Marylebone express. The gate on the right led to the brick yard. The British Railways Standard Class 5MT 4-6-0 was one of the standard classes of steam locomotives built by British Railways in the 1950s. 172 were built, essentially being a development of the LMS Stanier Class 5 4-6-0 ('Black Five'). The design work was done at the ex-LNER Doncaster Locomotive Drawing Office but the bulk of the construction was done at Derby Works.

Diesel-electric locomotive Type 4 no. D48 (later 45 038) with the up Waverley passing Westhouses and Blackwell signal box on 28 July 1967. The photograph was taken from Westhouses' Station road bridge, and in the distance Tibshelf Sidings can be seen. The British Rail Class 45 also known as the Sulzer Type 4 diesel locomotives were built by British Rail at their Derby and Crewe Works between 1960 and 1962. Along with the similar Class 44 and 46 locomotives, they became known as 'Peaks'. The Class 45s remained the main source of power on the Midland main line up to 1982, when they were relegated to secondary services following introduction of HSTs on the route. The great majority of Class 45s were withdrawn between 1981 and 1988 and the last was withdrawn from service by 1989 (*Diesel Loco Register* – S. A. Sugden).

Two

At City Stations

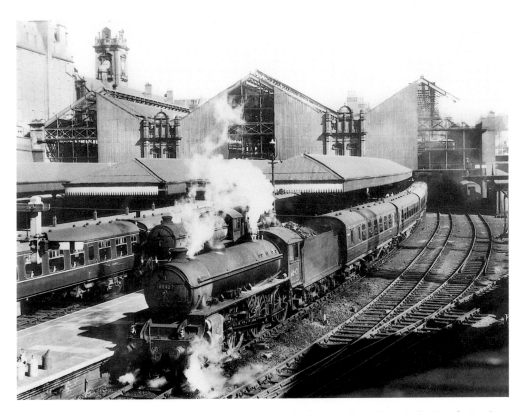

B1 Class 4-6-0 locomotive no. 61142 at the southern end of Nottingham Victoria Station during June 1965, with a Saturdays-only 09.55 Derby Friargate–Skegness train. The photograph was taken from Parliament Street Bridge. Nottingham Victoria was a Great Central Railway and Great Northern Railway station designed by the architect Albert Edward Lambert. It was opened by the Nottingham Joint Station Committee on 24 May 1900 and closed on 4 September 1967 by the London Midland Region of British Railways. The station building was mostly demolished and replaced by a shopping centre.

Royal Scot Class 4-6-0 locomotive no. 46167 *The Hertfordshire Regiment* leaving Nottingham Victoria Station with a southbound express parcels train. *wikepedia* states:

The station's construction was on a grand scale: a 13-acre (53,000 m²) site was acquired at a cost of £473,000 (£39.1 million as of 2010), in the heart of Nottingham's city centre; negotiations for the acquisition of the land had taken three years. The construction called for the demolition of whole streets of some 1,300 houses, 24 public houses and St. Stephen's Church, Bunker's Hill, following which around 600,000 cubic yards (460,000 m³) of sandstone was excavated from the site. The site measured around 650 yards (590 m) in length from north to south and had an average width of 110 yards (100 m) with a tunnel at each end of it for access.

A Darlington-built Class V2 2-6-2 locomotive no. 60961 takes water at the southern end of Nottingham Victoria Station's platform 10. The photograph was taken during April 1965 while the locomotive was working a York–Banbury fully fitted freight train.

Standing at Nottingham Victoria Station's no. 7 platform, on 29 May 1957, is B1 Class 4-6-0 locomotive no. 61177 with the up *South Yorkshireman* express. The train started at Bradford Exchange and engines were changed at Sheffield Victoria. A B1 allocated to Sheffield's Darnall Shed would then take the train through to Marylebone. An L1 Class locomotive may be seen on the right, with a local train to Grantham.

Ex-LMS Royal Scot Class 4-6-0 locomotive no. 46167 *The Hertfordshire Regiment* is at the station's southern end working a parcels train. The locomotive, built at Derby in 1930, was allocated to Annesley Shed when this photograph was taken in 1964. Note the turntable on the right.

Jubilee Class 4-6-0 locomotive no. 45653 *Barham* is in Nottingham Victoria Station with a parcels train. The main station building was in true Victorian splendour. It was constructed in a Renaissance style using the best quality faced bricks and Darley Dale stone with space at the front for Hackney carriages which was covered by a canopy. It faced on to the confluence of Mansfield Road and Milton Street for some 250 feet (76 m). The three-storey building was dominated by a large 100-foot (30 m) clock tower topped with a cupola and weather vane.

Leaving Victoria Station at Weekday Cross Junction with a Special Train is Jubilee Class 4-6-0 locomotive no. 45708 *Resolution*. Nottingham Victoria Station was officially opened without ceremony in the early hours of 24 May 1900 – over a year after the commencement of services on the new railway line. The first service to call at the station was a Great Central express from Manchester to Marylebone which pulled in at 1.12 a.m. It was followed fifteen minutes later by a Great Central express travelling in the opposite direction.

Royal Scot Class 4-6-0 locomotive no. 46112 *Sherwood Forester* at Nottingham Victoria Station with a parcels train. The last through service from Nottingham to London ran on 3 September 1966. All that was left was a DMU service between Nottingham and Rugby.

Having just arrived with empty coaches from New Basford Carriage Sidings, Jubilee Class 4-6-0 locomotive no. 45557 *New Brunswick* waits to depart from the southern end of Nottingham Victoria Station during August 1963, with the 17.15 to London Marylebone. To be seen in the top left corner of the picture is the clock tower situated at the front of the station. When the building was demolished the clock tower was preserved in front of the Victoria Shopping Centre.

A photograph showing the northern end of Nottingham Victoria Station during redevelopment.

Class J6 0-6-0 locomotive no. 64215 from Colwick, at the southern end of Nottingham Victoria Station, waiting to leave platform 9 on the 'roundabout' and infrequent service to Basford North via Gedling. It was known to local railwaymen as the 'round the houses' service.

Class D11/1 4-4-0 Large Director locomotive no. 62668 *Jutland* at Nottingham Victoria Station. The locomotive has just hauled the Sheffield Victoria–Nottingham Victoria local train and was waiting for the road to the turntable. The Sheffield Victoria–Nottingham Victoria locals called at Woodhouse, Killamarsh (Central), Renishaw (Central), Staveley (Central), Staveley Works, Chesterfied (Central), Heath, Pilsley, Tibshelf Town, Kirkby Bentinck, Hucknall Central and Bulwell Common. Fast trains on the route would omit Chesterfield and Staveley Works by taking the direct line between Staveley Town and Heath.

Class 0-6-0 J6 locomotive no. 64215 taking water at Nottingham Victoria Station, on 25 September 1957, before going on the turntable. A V2 can be seen in the bay platform. The station had passing loops round all platforms (for freight), two signal boxes and two turntables. The two signal boxes were positioned at the north and south ends of the station and controlled entry and exit to the tunnels that allowed entry to the complex. Traffic passing through was very varied including London–Manchester expresses, local services, cross-country services as well as freight workings.

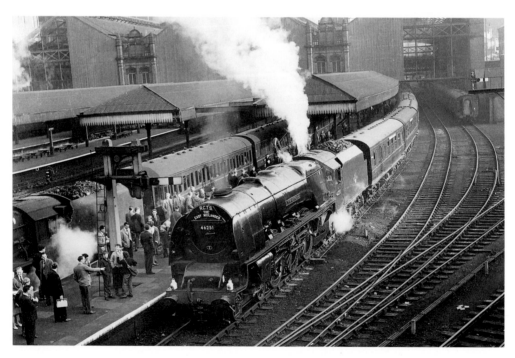

Duchess Class 4-6-2 locomotive no. 46251 *City of Nottingham* at the southern end of platform 10 of Nottingham Victoria Station, on 9 May 1964, with the RCTS East Midland Rail Tour. The train started from Nottingham Victoria, stopping at Didcot, Eastleigh and Swindon, before returning to Nottingham. The locomotive was withdrawn in 1964 and its nameplate is presently in Nottingham's Wollaton Hall Museum.

Class 1P locomotive on the goods line at the side of Nottingham Midland Station. The engine's fireman is believed to be George Sayles. Also visible is Class 4P 2-6-4T locomotive no. 42551. When the Great Central Railway opened its Victoria Station in 1900, the Midland Railway appointed Albert Edward Lambert, a local Nottingham architect, to rebuild the Midland Station. Lambert had been the architect for the Nottingham Victoria Railway Station and consequently the two buildings shared many similarities in their design.

About to leave Nottingham Midland Station during July 1961 is Jubilee Class 4-6-0 locomotive no. 45561 *Saskatchewan* with an excursion train to Dudley. The station was built in an Edwardian Baroque Revival style at a cost of £1 million (£79,620,000 as of 2010), and was described by the *Evening News* on the eve of its opening (16 January 1904) as a 'magnificent new block of buildings'.

Black Five 4-6-0 locomotive no. 44765 with double chimney (introduced 1947) is seen at the south end of Nottingham Midland Station during July 1964, with the 07.43 Nottingham Midland–Plymouth train. The lattice-work girder bridge carries the former GC main line across the station, but this has since been removed.

Crab Class 2-6-0 locomotive no. 42896 with the RCTS *East Midlander* leaving Nottingham Midland Station during October 1963 for Horwich Works. Driver H. Smith was in charge of the locomotive. The station's west box is visible on the left.

Class 2P 4-4-0 locomotive no. 40454 with the RCTS *East Midlander* Excursion – Nottingham Midland to Swindon rail tour on 6 May 1956. The men standing on the locomotive are, from left to right: John Henton (RCTS), Vic Forster (RCTS), driver George Kelsey, and fireman Jack Green.

Great Western 4-6-0 locomotive no. 4079 *Pendennis Castle* at Nottingham Midland, on 23 June 1972, before leaving for Market Overton. The seventh of the first lot of ten Castles built in 1923/24, no. 4079 *Pendennis Castle* was completed at Swindon Works in February 1924. After withdrawal in 1964 the locomotive, in time, was sold and shipped to Australia but has since returned and is preserved at the Didcot Railway Centre.

Pulling away from Nottingham Midland Station, on 11 March 1995, Class A4 locomotive no. 60009 *Union of South Africa* heads a John Player Special to Carlisle. The photograph was taken from a multi-storey car park near the station.

Class A3 4-6-2 locomotive no. 4472 *Flying Scotsman* leaving Nottingham Midland Station on 24 November 1984. The old goods warehouse, now demolished, can be seen in the background. The site now houses the city's law courts.

Just west of Nottingham Midland Station, on 10 July 1969, Class 47 locomotive no. D1629 is seen with a train of empties for a local colliery. The photograph also shows Nottingham Goods Yard East. The Class 47 (Originally Brush Type 4) was developed in the 1960s by Brush Traction. A total of 512 Class 47s were built at Crewe Works and Brush's Falcon Works, Loughborough, between 1962 and 1968.

Class 45 locomotive no. D106 arriving at Nottingham Midland Station, on 10 July 1969, with a St Pancras–Sheffield express train.

At Nottingham Midland Station, platform no. 6, on 2 July 1967, Class 40 locomotive D337 is with a parcels train.

A Class 08 locomotive is seen derailed at Nottingham Carriage Sidings.

Three

At Stations Around
the Area

Pinxton South Station was the terminus of a former GNR branch line which left the Nottingham–Derby Friargate line at Awsworth Junction, near Kimberley. Competition with bus services was always intense, trains taking forty minutes from Pinxton South to Nottingham, whereas the Midland General bus service took twenty-nine minutes for the same journey. The result was inevitable and the line closed on 1 January 1963. The photograph was taken just after Bill had heard about the imminent closure of the line. The overbridge in the background carried a road across the Midland Railway's Pye Bridge–Kirby-in-Ashfield line. It is presently part of the M1 motorway.

Above and below: Colwick Shed provided the motive power to run on the line to Pinxton South and these photographs show one of the Class L1 locomotives regularly used on the service. Class L1 2-6-4T locomotive no. 67787 is seen on 25 June 1962, before and after running round its train. These locomotives were designed by Edward Thompson.

At Bulwell Common Station, on 19 August 1956, Class N7/3 0-6-2T locomotive no. 69692 is with the 'DIDO'(day-in-day-out) service, running from Bulwell Common down the former GN line, to Newstead Station. On Saturdays it ran to Annesley Station on the GC main line. The DIDO finished on 10 September 1962; the last locomotives used were BR Standard Tanks. Bulwell Common Station was closed to passengers and goods on 4 March 1963, the line itself on 5 September 1966 to passengers and completely on 25 March 1968. Where the station once stood is now a housing development, but the stationmaster's house remains.

At Bulwell Common Station, on 12 June 1956, is Class C12 4-4-2T locomotive no. 67363 with the DIDO. On the left a driver walks along the platform to catch the train. There was basically a train every hour. The station at Annesley was only a wooden platform. On the right is the down siding with a water column and in the distance Bulwell Common South Junction Box can be seen.

With the 13.32 from Basford North to Nottingham Victoria via Gedling, Class K3/2 2-6-0 – Gresley locomotive no. 61974 passes through Daybrook Station on the old GNR line on 12 March 1958. The line between Basford and Gedling was closed some time later. The closure was hastened by the serious condition of Mapperley Tunnel (1,132 yards long), caused by mining subsidence. Daybrook Station had been closed since 14 September 1931.

Here we see the Southwell to Rolleston Junction push-pull train at Southwell Station on 20 August 1958. The entire line was from Rolleston to Mansfield but the passenger service beyond Southwell had ceased some time earlier. The Rolleston–Southwell service ceased on 15 June 1959.

Above and below: Class 1P 0-4-4T locomotive no. 58065 at Southwell Station, on 20 August 1958, before leaving for Rolleston Junction. The route beyond the station for Farsfield is now a nature walk. *wikepedia* states:

> Southwell once had a railway station on a branch line of the Midland Railway, running from Mansfield to Rolleston Junction, a station on the Nottingham–Lincoln Line. When the station was rebuilt in 1871, the platform shelters and the station master's house were dismantled and rebuilt at Beeston where they survive today at Beeston railway station. The Mansfield to Southwell section, which passed through a mining area, was an early casualty, passenger services terminating in 1959, with freight ending as part of the Dr Beaching cuts in 1964.

View from Trent Station looking towards Trent Station North Box. On the extreme left was the North Curve. Behind the signal box is the Erewash line. The direct line is to Nottingham. The railway cottages are still extant today and the large house was occupied by the station master.

Heading in the Leicester direction, with a fully fitted frieght train past Trent Station North Junction Box, is Class 5MT locomotive no. 42816.

At the northern end of Trent Station during May 1960, Royal Scot Class 4-6-0 locomotive no. 46139 *The Welsh Regiment* is seen with a St Pancras–Bradford train. The line to the right led to Sawley Junction (known as North Curve). Trent was a junction station in the middle of nowhere. Probably 95 per cent of the passengers changed trains there, without leaving the station; it closed on 1 January 1968.

Heading a Derby Friargate–Nottingham Victoria local train, on 30 August 1963, at West Hallam Station, is 4MT locomotive no. 43154. Note the colliery headstock in the background. *wikepedia* notes the following interesting snippets of information about the station:

[It] was originally called Stanley, but its name was quickly changed to West Hallam for Dale Abbey to avoid confusion with another station in West Yorkshire. It was provided with substantial brick buildings; a two-storey station master's house and the usual single storey offices on the main platform with a small timber waiting room on the other. It was one of the few intermediate stations on the line to have a footbridge, due to an elderly couple having been killed by a light engine in 1884. Beside the presence of productive collieries, it was particularly busy during World War II due to a nearby ordnance depot, a satellite of that at Chilwell. Sunday passengers services finished in 1939, and it closed completely in 1964.

Four

On Shed

Posing for the camera are engine cleaners at Nottingham Midland Shed. On the left is the cleaning foreman and next to him is the shed foreman. The Jubilee Class 4-6-0 engine was working a 1957 Raleigh Works outing.

At Colwick Shed, Jubilee Class 4-6-0 locomotive no. 45562 *Alberta* pauses before working the Nottingham Midland–Bradford train. Note the ash pits in the foreground. The locomotive saw thirty-four years' service between being built by the North British Locomotive Company, Glasgow, in 1934, and withdrawal in October 1967. Its last shed allocation was 20A Leeds Holbeck. The Jubilee locomotives were designed for main line passenger work.

Pictured alongside the old oil tanks, at Colwick Shed, on 12 July 1952, is Class B16/1 4-6-0 locomotive no. 61426. The North Eastern Railway Class S3, classified B16 by the LNER, was a class of 4-6-0 steam locomotive designed for mixed-traffic work. It was designed by Vincent Raven, with Stephenson valve gear inside, and introduced in 1920. The locomotives passed to the London & North Eastern Railway (LNER) in 1923 and some of them were rebuilt as B16/2 (introduced 1937, LNER rebuild of B16/1 by Nigel Gresley with Gresley conjugated valve gear) or B16/3 (introduced 1944, LNER rebuild of B16/1 by Edward Thompson with three sets of Walschaerts valve gear). The picture was taken by Bill on a Sunday visit.

Seen fully coaled at Colwick, Jubilee Class 4-6-0 locomotive no. 45581 *Bihar and Orissa* is running light engine to Nottingham. The majority of the Jubilee Class engines were nameless at first, but eventually they were all named: eighty-six after names from the British Empire, thirty-nine admirals, eight sea battles, forty-four ships of the line, eight early steam locomotive names and the four provinces of Ireland completing the selection. It was not until 1938 that the final loco was named, all but one of the final sixty-three being named from new.

Passing the coal hopper at Colwick, Jubilee Class 4-6-0 locomotive no. 45647 *Sturdee* is running light engine to the shed after working from Bradford to Nottingham. Built at Crewe Works, the William A. Stanier-designed locomotive was in service between 1935 and 1967.

Class 04/5 2-8-0 locomotive no. 63628 is filling with coal under the hopper at Colwick Shed on 19 April 1955.

Pictured at Colwick Shed, on 19 April 1955, is Class A5/1 4-6-2T locomotive no. 69818 (pre-Grouping GCR 374). The Robinson-designed locomotive was built at Gorton Works in 1917 and withdrawn in December 1958. The last shed allocation was 38B Annesley. A total of forty-four Class A5 engines were built, thirty-one by Robinson (Class A5/1) and thirteen by Gresley (Class A5/2).

As a photographer, Bill states that Colwick was a difficult shed to sneak round taking pictures – even when he was BR staff. However, he was successful during April 1965 when taking this picture of Class 04/1 2-8-0 locomotive no. 63707 near the ash pits. Another problem for a photographer was posed by the electric lamp standards around the area. It was difficult to take a picture without it appearing as if the lamps were 'growing' from, or attached to, some part of the locomotive.

The J6s were known to ex-GN crews as the A Class, and one of the 0-6-0 locomotives, no. 64273, is pictured at Colwick Shed on 15 April 1958. The first fifteen J6 locomotives were built to Ivatt's design (Great Northern Railway 521 series) and the remainder to a design which was slightly modified by Gresley (and designated 536 series) after he became CME of the GNR in 1911. The London & North Eastern Railway classified them both as J6 and they were used for goods traffic. 110 locomotives passed to British Railways in 1948 and they were numbered 64170–64279. None are preserved. No. 64273 emerged from Doncaster Works in 1922 and lasted until December 1959. Its last shed allocation was 38A Colwick.

Another image from the batch Bill took at Colwick Shed in April 1958 was this one of Class J94 0-6-0ST locomotive no. 68033. The Class of J94s, totalling seventy-five, was introduced by Robert Riddles, based on a Hunslett design, and built 1943-45. Withdrawals commenced in 1960, the last two, nos 68006 and 68012 were withdrawn in 1967 on closure of the Crompton & High Peak Railway.

Class N5/2 0-6-2T locomotive no. 69286 at Colwick Shed on 15 April 1955. In the background is one of the engine sheds.

Approaching Mansfield South Junction, on 10 October 1964 with the old Mansfield Midland Shed on the left, is Class 4F 0-6-0 locomotive no. 44376. The photograph was taken from the footbridge. The locomotive was running light engine to Kirkby Shed. No. 44376 was built in 1927 by Andrew Barclay, Sons & Co. Ltd, Kilmarnock, and its last shed allocation was 16C Kirkby in Ashfield before withdrawal in December 1964.

At Nottingham Midland Shed, on 8 February 1950, is Class 4MT locomotive no. 43040 with double chimney. The LMS Ivatt Class 4 2-6-0 was a class of steam locomotive primarily designed for medium freight work but also widely used on secondary passenger services. 162 were built between 1947 and 1952, of these only three were built by the LMS before nationalisation in 1948. Designed by H. G. Ivatt, they were classified 4F by the LMS and 4MT by BR. The photograph was taken on a Sunday visit.

Class LYR27 – 3F (Ex-L&YR) 0-6-0 locomotive no. 52135 (rebuilt with Belpaire boiler), at Nottingham Midland Shed on 8 February 1950. The locomotive was designed by Aspinall and built at Horwich Works in 1891, surviving until November 1959.

Ex-LMS *Royal Scot* Class 4-6-0 locomotive no. 46112 *Sherwood Forester* at the Wilford Road end of Nottingham Midland no. 3 shed. The picture was taken on 12 August 1961. The London, Midland & Scottish Railway (LMS) *Royal Scot* Class is a class of 4-6-0 express passenger locomotive introduced in 1927. Originally having parallel boilers, all members were later rebuilt with tapered type 2A boilers, and were in effect two classes. The class title of *Royal Scot* was subsequently reused in 1976 as an official name for the then-new Class 87s but it never stuck, and was withdrawn partly out of respect for the original fleet. *Sherwood Forester* was built in 1927, rebuilt with a tapered boiler in 1943 and withdrawn from Annesley Shed in September 1964. The buildings in the background include outdoor machine shops.

Inside Nottingham Midland no. 3 shed. Among those on the right are: driver 'Dad Stevo', Harry Martin and the shed foreman. The locomotives in the background include two Black Fives.

Standing on Toton Shed near the coaling plant on 30 October 1955, is Class 9F locomotive no. 92020, as built with Crosti boiler. The Class 9F was the last in a series of standardised locomotive classes designed for British Railways during the 1950s, and was intended for use on fast, heavy freight trains over long distances. It was one of the most powerful steam locomotive types ever constructed in Britain, and successfully performed its intended duties. At various times during the 1950s, the 9Fs worked passenger trains with great success, indicating the versatility of the design, sometime considered to represent the ultimate in British steam development. Several variants were constructed for experimentation purposes in an effort to reduce costs and maintenance, although these met with varying degrees of success. The total number built was 251, production being shared between Swindon (53) and Crewe Works (198). Ten locomotives (numbers 92020–92029) were built in 1955 with the Franco-Crosti boiler. Withdrawals of the Class 9F began in 1964, with the final locomotives removed from service in 1968. Several examples have survived into the preservation era in varying states of repair, including *Evening Star*.

Diesel-electric Class 25/2 locomotive no. D5240 at Nottingham Shed, on 27 March 1965, with driver Ken Wilcox in the cab. The British Rail Class 25 diesel locomotives were known as Sulzer Type 2 and nicknamed 'Rats', as it was alleged they could be seen everywhere in Britain, and hence were 'as common as rats'. In total, 327 locomotives of this type were built between 1961 and 1967. The Class 25/2 locomotives (number sequence (original) D5233–D5299, D7500–D7597 (TOPS) 25 083–25 247) featured restyled bodywork and two-tone green livery similar to that carried by the Brush Type 4 (Class 47). The majority were built at BR Derby although some came out of the Darlington works.

Leaving Toton down sidings, on 30 October 1955, with a train of empties, is Class 2-6-0 0-6-2T Beyer Garratt locomotive no. 47998. The coal hopper at Toton Shed is visible.

Interior of Toton Shed; the locomotives include a 3F, 8F, two Jintys and a Garratt in the background.

Class OF 0-4-0ST locomotive no. 41518 at Toton Shed on 30 October 1955. These locomotives were suitable for brewery work around Burton-on-Trent or in the steel works at Barrow Hill. The shed at Toton was replaced by a Diesel Maintenance Depot. The OF Class, designed by Johnson, was built 1883-1903. Twenty three locos survived the Grouping in 1923, but most had disappeared before 1930. No. 41518 was built at Derby Works in 1893 and survived until February 1958; the last shed allocation was 24D Lower Darwen.

In an appropriately named section of Toton Shed called Garratt Alley, Class 2-6-0 0-6-2T Beyer Garratt locomotive no. 47981 is seen on 11 March 1956. At this point the locomotive was only months away from withdrawal in November of that year. Its last shed allocation was 18A Toton.

Diesel-electric Sulzer Type 4 locomotive no. D1 *Scafell Pike* (later 44001) and D5 *Cross Fell* at Toton Diesel Depot. The British Rail Class 44 or Sulzer Type 4 diesel locomotives were built by British Railways' Derby Works between 1959 and 1960. They were named after British mountains, and consequently nicknamed 'Peaks'. *Scafell Pike* was withdrawn in October 1976 and scrapped at Derby in February 1977. *Cross Fell* was withdrawn in April 1978 and scrapped at Derby in November in the same year.

Class 4F 0-6-0 – Fowler locomotive no. 44218 on the ash pits at Westhouses Shed on 18 July 1966. In the background is the old coal stage. Built by the Midland Railway, the engine shed included arrival and departure roads, an ash road, six internal roads and the legs road, which once had a shear legged crane positioned over it. This was used for the lifting of locomotives. The shed closed to locomotives when traffic defects caused a Class 56 to derail and the shed was deemed to be no longer in a usable condition. Operations were moved to Tibshelf Sidings until the complete closure of Westhouses as a train crew depot in January 1987.

Class 4-6-0 Black Five – Stanier locomotive no. 44743, built with Caprotti valve gear, at Westhouses Shed on 15 April 1965. The London Midland & Scottish Railway's Class 5 4-6-0, almost universally known as the Black Five, was introduced by William Stanier in 1934 and 842 were built between then and 1951. Members of the class survived to the last day of steam on British Railways in 1968 and eighteen are preserved.

Five

Crash at Lenton

On 16 December 1971, at about 06.15, two drivers and a guard were killed at Lenton South Junction, Nottingham. A special freight train, double-headed by Class 20 locomotives nos D8115 and D8142, and conveying coal from Bestwood Park Sidings to Derby Gas Works, was running off the up north curve line through Lenton South Junction on to the up main line, under clear signals, when it was struck head-on by the 01.30 parcels train hauled by Class 25 locomotive no. D7605 from Liverpool (Lime Street) to Nottingham. The latter train, running on the down main line, had passed at danger, the signal protecting the junction. The collision happened before dawn, in fine weather and good visibility.

The locomotives of both trains were derailed and badly damaged. Five vehicles of the coal train and four of the parcels train were derailed. The lines were cleared using the Toton steam cranes.

A railway official praised the action of the coal train guard, in jumping from his van and placing detonators on the line. The Derby to Nottingham line was blocked and London-bound express was cancelled. Others were diverted and local passengers were taken into Nottingham by bus.

Six

Industrial Locomotives

A scene at Williamsthorpe Colliery, on 19 October 1967, where Class 3F 0-6-0T – Fowler, locomotives nos 47383 and 47629 were the last steam workings in the area. The locomotives were maintained at Westhouses Shed. No. 47383 was built at Vulcan Foundry in 1926 and withdrawn in December 1967; no. 47629 was built at Beardmore, Dalmuir, Glasgow, in 1928, surviving until October 1967.

A narrow gauge locomotive, Beeston no. 1, built in 1889 by William Bagnall, is at Beeston Creosote Sidings on 25 March 1967. This was an area situated between Lenton South Junction and Beeston, where railway sleepers were creosoted. Standard gauge locomotives also operated in the sidings. The area is now the site of Nottingham's Freightliner Depot.

NCB locomotive 0-4-0ST *Lancaster* at Bestwood Colliery during 1955. The locomotive was built in 1888 by Peckett, works no. 468. Bestwood Colliery closed in 1967.

NCB 0-6-0ST Felix, built by A. Barclay & Co. in 1954, works no. 2344, is pictured at Bestwood Colliery in 1967.

Class Y7 0-4-0T locomotive no. 68088 at Bentinck Colliery Shed. Later the locomotive went to Priory Farm and Thurgarton Farm, then to Ruddington Heritage Centre.

Boots' Beeston Sidings, where Boots' no. 2 locomotive, built by A. Barclay in 1935 (works no. 2008), can be seen.

Brookhill Colliery, Pinxton, during August 1967, where Emfour no. 2 is working. The 0-6-0ST locomotive was built by Hudswell Clarke & Co. in 1954, works no. 1877.

NCB locomotive *Felix* at Bestwood Colliery in August 1967. The locomotive was built by A. Barclay in 1954, works no. 2344.

Calverton Colliery Sidings, where contractors McAlpine & Co's locomotive, ex-LMS no. 11257 L&Y Pug Tank, is helping to lay a new siding for BR trains. Calverton Colliery was started in 1937 but with the intervention of the Second World War did not open until 1952. It closed in 1993 but was reopened by RJB Mining, eventually shutting for good in 1999.

A 0-6-0ST locomotive no. 7285 *Michael* at Cinderhill Colliery in 1949. The locomotive was built by Robert Stephenson & Hawthorn in 1945. Cinderhill (or Babbington) Colliery was sunk in 1840-41 and was the first pit in the Notts concealed coal seam. After the pit closed in 1986, the Phoenix Business Centre was developed on the site.

0-6-0ST locomotive *King George* at Gedling Colliery on 12 May 1970. The locomotive, built in 1942, was photographed when out of use, being replaced by a diesel. It is presently preserved at Toddington. Gedling Colliery (which was once the life blood of Gedling and many of the other surrounding villages), opened in 1899 and closed in 1991.

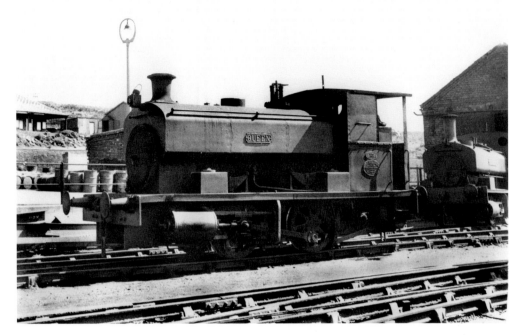

NCB 0-4-0ST locomotive no. 1784 *Queen* at Gedling Colliery. The locomotive was built by A. Barclay & Co. in 1923.

Pictured at Gedling Colliery on 30 January 1955 is NCB 0-6-0ST locomotive no. 1253 *Audrey*, built by Peckett & Co. in 1911.

At Hucknall Colliery, on 10 July 1949, is NCB locomotive no. 1440 *Sherwood* no. 3, built by Manning Wardle & Co. in 1899. The Hucknall Colliery Company, formed in 1861, sank two shafts: Hucknall no. 1 colliery (known as 'Top Pit') in 1861 (off Watnall Road) and Hucknall no. 2 colliery (known as 'Bottom Pit') in 1866 (off Portland Road). No. 1 closed by 1943, and no. 2 closed in 1986.

Kitson & Co. of Leeds built this 0-6-0ST locomotive in 1874, works no. 1996. It is pictured (ex-Barber Walker & Co.) as NCB no. 5 at Moorgreen Colliery. The mine was first sunk in 1865 and was closed in 1985.

NCB 0-6-0ST locomotive *Peter* at Linby Colliery during August 1967. It was built at Hunslet & Co., Leeds, in 1943, works no. 2853 (formerly WD 75004).

Pinxton Colliery Shed on 18 June 1955. On the left is NCB 0-6-0T locomotive no. 1877 *Emfour* no. 2, built by Hudswell Clarke & Co. in 1954. On the right is NCB 0-6-0T *Emfour* no. 4, also built by Hudswell Clarke & Co. in 1954, works no. 1879.

Pinxton Colliery, 25 May 1962, showing NCB 0-4-ST locomotive no. 1975 *Peckett* no. 2, built by Peckett & Co. in 1939 (rebuilt 1958).

Shown at William Rigley's Wagon Works, Bulwell Forest, on 10 July 1949, is 0-4-0ST locomotive *Stanlow*, built by Manning Wardle & Co. in 1887, works no. 1017. Keith Allen is pictured in the cab, while Peter Elson is on the right.

Class O2/3 2-8-0 – Gresley locomotive no. 63964 waits to be scrapped at Rigley's Wagon Works on 19 January 1964. The locomotive emerged from Doncaster Works in 1942 and was withdrawn in 1964; the last shed allocation was 36E Retford (GC). The O2/3 Class was a post-grouping development of Gresley O2/2 with detail differences, reduced boiler mountings and side window cabs. None are preserved.

Being dismantled at Rigley's Wagon Works on 28 August 1964, is Class K1 2-6-0 locomotive no. 62013. Designed by Peppercorn the K1's proved to be useful and versatile engines. They worked extensively over ex-LNER territory but were chiefly associated with north east England and like so many post-nationalisation classes the K1's had relatively brief lives. All were withdrawn between 1962 and 1967, but the last to be retired managed to escape the cutter's torch; no. 62005 *Lord of the Isles* is preserved by North Eastern Locomotive Preservation Group (NELPG).

Built by the Avondale Engine Co. in 1909, works no. 1567, locomotive *Stanton* no. 3 is working at Stanton Iron Works on 14 August 1955.

0-6-0ST NCB locomotive *Sherwood* at Sherwood Colliery. The locomotive was built by A. Barclay & Co., Kilmarnock, in 1922, works no. 1638. Sherwood Colliery existed *c*. 1902-92.

At Stanton Iron Works on 14 August 1955 is 0-6-0ST locomotive *Stanton* no. 15, built by the Avonside Engine Co. in 1902, works no. 1457.

Working at Summit Colliery, Kirkby, in August 1967, is NCB 0-6-0ST locomotive no. 33 (formerly *Swannick* no. 4 at Kirkby Colliery from 1957). The engine was built by Peckett & Co. in 1936, works no. 1902. Summit Colliery was officially called Kirkby Colliery, originally owned by the Butterley Company and sunk in 1883. It closed in 1968 with the loss of over 1,000 jobs. In its hey day the pit was a large employer in the area, having a brick yard and a railway attached to it.

Working at Williamsthorpe Colliery is Class 3F-F 0-6-0T – Fowler locomotive no. 47629. The locomotive was on loan to the NCB from Westhouses Shed.

Watnall open cast plant on 30 September 1955, with NCB 0-6-0T locomotive no. 8416, formerly ex-LNER no. 8416.

Seven

Portraits and Groups

Inside Nottingham London Road Junction Box, with signalman Ron Astel.

Left: Fred Cassidy of Nottingham on the footplate of a Class 8F 2-8-0 locomotive.

Below: Driver George Perrons on the footplate of a Class 8F 2-8-0 locomotive.

Right: Driver George Perrons oiling
Class 8F 2-8-0 locomotive no. 48614.

Below: Nottingham driver Jack Radford
at the controls of a Class 45 diesel-electric
locomotive.

Driver George Chambers at the controls of a Class 47 diesel-electric locomotive.

On the footplate of an 8F 2-8-0 locomotive with driver Reg Gascoigne.

Class A3 4-6-2 – Gresley locomotive no. 4472 *Flying Scotsman* at Nottingham Holding Sidings, 29 March 1974.

Nottingham Shed outing to Crewe Works.

At the helm of a Class 45 diesel-electric locomotive en route to St Pancras is driver E. Noel.

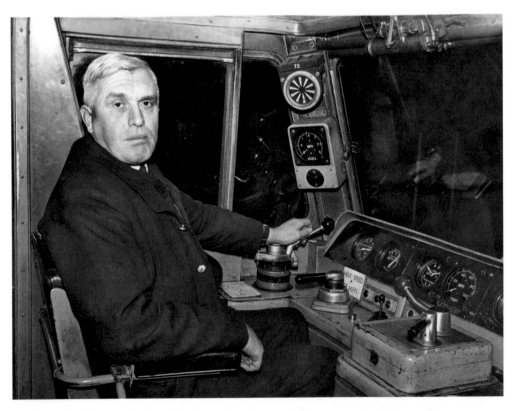

In charge of a Class 47 diesel-electric locomotive is H. Smith, known as 'Fire-Eater Smith'.